THOMAS KINKADE

Painter of Light ™

Our Family

Through the Generations

THOMAS NELSON, INC.
Nashville, TN 37214

Our Family

Through the Generations

We are shaped by the times in which we live, and we all carry with us little pieces of each of the generations that came before us.

Who in the generations of your family had a great love for music, or art? Where has that love reappeared in future generations?

Did the times they lived in encourage those passions, or were they lost to practical needs and struggles. Perhaps creativity took on other forms . . . cooking, sewing, gardening or building furniture. Who now carries on those traditions in your family?

Use this book to help preserve the treasured history of your family's generations.

Interview grandparents, parents and other family members and friends. You will be surprised at how different they were when they were young, and how they will remind you of someone in your family today.

As you complete the book, encourage them to tell you stories about the times they lived in when they were growing up, how they see the world as having changed. Compare their stories to how you look at the world you live in today, and how it is changing for the next generation coming up.

Our Family's Heritage

*I*magine the courage it took, often at a very young age, to leave behind family and the everyday world you know, and travel to an unknown place to start a new life. Our family came to America bringing with them what they could carry in their hearts, a spirit of adventure and hope for the future.

Our family came from

_____

Their home there was

_____

_____

They earned a living as

_____

_____

They came to America because

_____

_____

_____

_____

Coming to America

Picture a place where you're yearning to be. –THOMAS KINKADE

The first in the family to come to America were _____

The year they came was approximately _____

Their ages when they traveled were _____

They traveled by _____

Who they left behind _____

The first to arrive in America settled in _____

Their home was _____

They earned a living by _____

Stories about their early life in America _____

A Glimpse into Yesterday

GRANDPARENTS' GENERATION

*F*amily ties are kept strong by learning about our ancestors and learning from them.

Memorable events in their lifetime were

_____
_____
_____
_____

How society changed during their lifetime

_____
_____
_____
_____

People who influenced their generation were

_____
_____
_____
_____

Ways life was harder then

_____
_____
_____
_____

Inventions and discoveries in their lifetime

_____
_____
_____
_____

Ways the world was better then

_____
_____
_____
_____

The Branches of Our Tree

MATERNAL GRANDMOTHER AND GRANDFATHER

We were made for calm, not chaos, and that is why we long for simpler times. –THOMAS KINKADE

Grandmother's name _____

We called her _____

She was born on _____

in _____

She grew up in _____

Her faith _____

Her education _____

Grandma worked as _____

_____

She loved to _____

_____

_____

_____

Grandfather's name _____

We called him _____

He was born on _____

in _____

He grew up in _____

His faith _____

His education _____

Grandfather worked as _____

_____

He loved to _____

_____

_____

_____

(PLACE PHOTO HERE)

A Lifetime Remembered

THEIR LIFE TOGETHER

The greatest thing in life is to be needed. – THOMAS KINKADE

They were married on _____

They had _____ children named _____

Places they traveled to
_____
_____
_____
_____

Hardships they faced were
_____
_____

My favorite memories
_____
_____
_____
_____
_____
_____
_____
_____
_____
_____
_____
_____
_____

They enjoyed doing these things together
_____
_____
_____
_____
_____

(PLACE PHOTO HERE)

The Circle Continues

PATERNAL GRANDMOTHER AND GRANDFATHER

Loving and giving go hand in hand. –THOMAS KINKADE

Grandfather's name _____

We called him _____

He was born on _____

in _____

He grew up in _____

His faith _____

His education _____

Grandfather worked as _____

He loved to _____

(PLACE PHOTO HERE)

Grandmother's name _____

We called her _____

She was born on _____

in _____

She grew up in _____

Her faith _____

Her education _____

Grandma worked as _____

She loved to _____

Hearth and Home

THEIR LIFE TOGETHER

Surround yourself with what you love. –THOMAS KINKADE

They were married on _____

They had _____ children named _____

Places they traveled to

_____

_____

_____

Hardships they faced were

_____

_____

_____

My favorite memories

_____

_____

_____

_____

_____

_____

_____

_____

_____

They enjoyed doing these things together

_____

_____

_____

(PLACE PHOTO HERE)

The Fabric of Our Family

OUR PARENTS' GENERATION

Memorable events in their lifetime were

_____

_____

_____

_____

How society changed during their lifetime

_____

_____

_____

_____

People who influenced their generation were

_____

_____

_____

Ways life was harder then

_____

_____

_____

Inventions and discoveries in their lifetime

_____

_____

_____

(PLACE PHOTO HERE)

Ways the world was better then

_____

_____

_____

_____

A Legacy of Love

ABOUT MY MOTHER

Your family is a gift you have been given. –THOMAS KINKADE

My mother's name _____

She was born on _____

in _____

She grew up in _____

Her faith _____

Her education _____

Her career _____

Her favorite pastimes _____

The best advice she ever gave me _____

My favorite memories _____

(PLACE PHOTO HERE)

Guiding the Way

ABOUT MY FATHER

A family's love makes a house a home. –THOMAS KINKADE

My father's name _____

He was born on _____

in _____

He grew up in _____

His faith _____

His education _____
_____
_____

His career _____
_____
_____
_____

His favorite pastimes _____
_____
_____

The best advice he ever gave me _____
_____
_____

My favorite memories _____
_____
_____
_____
_____
_____
_____
_____
_____

(PLACE PHOTO HERE)

Life's Treasured Moments

FAMILY LIFE

Stories about our family life

My parents were married on _____

at _____

When they were married, mother was _____ years old. Dad was _____.

When they were first married, they lived in _____

Later they lived in _____

They had _____ children named _____

_____

_____

_____

(PLACE PHOTO HERE)

They were proud of _____

_____

_____

_____

The Story Continues

MY GENERATION

I was born in _____

Memorable events in my lifetime
_____
_____
_____
_____
_____
_____
_____

How society has changed during my lifetime
_____
_____
_____
_____
_____
_____
_____
_____

People who influenced my generation
_____
_____
_____
_____

Ways life was harder when I was growing up
_____
_____
_____

Inventions and discoveries in my lifetime
_____
_____
_____
_____

Ways the world was better then
_____
_____
_____
_____
_____

(PLACE PHOTO HERE)

Home is Where the Heart is

CHILDHOOD HOME

Glowing windows say welcome... someone waiting cares enough
to leave the light on... –THOMAS KINKADE

Our family consisted of

_____

_____

We lived in

_____

_____

What mealtimes were like in our family

_____

_____

Hobbies and games we played

_____

_____

Special places I loved to go to

_____

_____

_____

Friends and relatives we saw often

_____

_____

Trips we took

_____

_____

_____

People I turned to for advice

_____

_____

Memorable advice I was given

_____

_____

_____

Family Traditions

Like a circle with no beginning and no end, traditions connect us to our past and future.

Celebrate life everyday. – THOMAS KINKADE

Some of our family traditions

_____
_____
_____
_____
_____
_____

Holiday traditions

_____
_____
_____
_____
_____

The holidays our family celebrates are

_____
_____
_____
_____
_____

Traditional foods we serve at the holidays

_____
_____
_____
_____
_____
_____

The Tie that Binds

OUR FAITH

Faith is a constant thread strengthening the fabric of our family. – THOMAS KINKADE

Where we worship _____

How our faith has influenced our family _____

Our religious traditions through the generations _____

Special celebrations of our faith _____

Let Your Light Shine

CREATIVITY

Creativity takes many forms...painting, cooking, writing, inventing. Its seeds are passed down from generation to generation.

Creativity is one of the great privileges of being human. –THOMAS KINKADE

My grandparents showed their creativity by

_____

_____

_____

Others in their generation and their talents

_____

_____

My parents were creative at

_____

_____

_____

Others in my parents' generation and their talents

_____

_____

_____

_____

_____

My generation shows their creativity in

_____

_____

_____

_____

_____

A Recipe for Love

FAMILY RECIPES

Food can be an expression of love and a celebration of heritage. When shared with a loved one it is a sumptuous feast. –THOMAS KINKADE

Favorite Family Stories

These special stories are a glimpse into our family's past.

Fill your home with love and laughter. –THOMAS KINKADE

THOMAS KINKADE, the celebrated *Painter of Light™*, is the most collected living artist in America today. His paintings with their glowing windows and tranquil settings are collected throughout the world, inviting us to reflect back upon simpler times and the sanctity of home and family. Kinkade is a devoted husband and father, and lives with his wife Nanette and their four daughters in Northern California.

THOMAS KINKADE'S PAINTINGS